God's Little Sunflower

When a Child Dies

by P. A. Miller

Copyright © 2009 by P. A. Miller

God's Little Sunflower
When a Child Dies
by P. A. Miller

Printed in the United States of America

ISBN 978-1-60791-498-3

All rights reserved solely by the author. The author guarantees all contents are original and do not infringe upon the legal rights of any other person or work. No part of this book may be reproduced in any form without the permission of the author. The views expressed in this book are not necessarily those of the publisher.

Unless otherwise indicated, Bible quotations are taken from The Biblegateway.com., Copyright © 1995-2009 by The Zondervan Corporation, and The New International Version (NIV), Copyright © 1973, 1978, 1984 by International Bible Society, and The Today's New International Version (TNIV), Copyright © 2001, 2005 by International Bible Society, and The New King James Version (NKJV), Copyright © 1982 by Thomas Nelson, Inc., and The King James Version (KJV) Public Domain.

www.xulonpress.com

God's Little Sunflower

Written by a grieving grandmother

***Dedicated to the loving memory
of Diovanni Nevaeh***

*Trust in the Lord with all your heart
and lean not on your own understanding; In all your ways
acknowledge Him,
and He shall direct your paths.*

Proverbs 3: 5-6 (NKJV)

The Sunflower

**Tall, graceful, beautiful wildflowers
They turn and face the sun, no matter what . . . .
May we learn to turn and face the Son, no matter what . . .**

*My darling Diovanni,
I love you, but Jesus loves you best.*

*Love,
Nana*

Thank you . . . . .

God, for Your comfort. You are the anchor I cling to.

My husband, for being there the best you knew how. May you continue to seek Him.

Mom, for your prayers. May God continue to bless you on your life's journey.

Sandra, for your presence on center stage. I will be forever grateful to you.

Chaplain Von (Pa Pa), for guiding me as I crawled through the darkest days of my life. You are truly a gift from God.

My family and friends near and far, for the kind words of compassion.

Susan, Ann, and Robert—my miracle friends from Wimberley, Texas. Your words of comfort will stay with me always.

My military family, for many prayers, kind words, generous gifts, and overwhelming support. You came through when I needed you the most.

Everyone who knew her, held her, prayed for her, laughed with, and loved her for the brief time she was here. She has touched all of us.

Thank you. I love you all.

Contents

To the reader.. xiii

Words from a fragile heart................................... xv

i grieve..17
i 19
why..20
i cry 21
another day...22
the darkness..23
still...25

i accept..27
everywhere i go...28
God's garden 30
gone 2 soon 32
miss you 33
you never know 34

i reflect 35
reflections 36
never got to 38
smile 39
this summer 41
the special pink box 43

i write 45
journal entries 45

i survive 73
who is that lady? 74
special words 75

Words from a humbled heart 81

About the author 85

Dear Reader,

Sitting in the front row at a funeral service . . . staring at the tiny casket which held my two-year-old granddaughter's body . . . a moment that will be forever engraved on my soul. Chances are if you are reading this, your life has been changed due to the death of a child. Perhaps you will identify with some of the words expressed during the rawness of the grief. Perhaps you will find something in this book to identify with where you are, where you hope to be.

My prayer in sharing my grief is to show you how God was there comforting and encouraging me as I *walked through the darkest days of my life. I would experience another soul-engraving moment twenty-three months later, sitting, once again in the front row, now at the funeral service of my only child.** When my life once again shattered into pieces, He was there. He is always there. I have learned to depend on Him. I have learned to trust Him, no matter what. I have learned to praise the God who gives . . . and takes away. My hope is that you will see no matter how dark the circumstances, there is hope. There is hope in Jesus Christ. Trust Him.*

P.A.Miller

**see note on "Words from a Humbled Heart" page (83)

Words from a fragile heart

I wasn't ever excited about the thought of one day becoming a grandmother. I thought that label would make me seem or feel much older than I really was. Then I held her in my arms. The world was more colorful when she was around. Life exuded from her. She embraced love. Every moment with her truly engraved, in pure gold, that special bond between us. The past heartaches in my life all seemed worthwhile due to the one single fact that she existed. She existed here in this world. For twenty-five beautiful months she was here.

Then the phone call.

Not breathing. Brain damage. Doesn't look good. Not coming back from this. Praying. Crying. Pleading. What happened? How did we get here? Tiny white casket. Size-two dress. Pink roses. Can't believe I'm here. Viewing. Numb. Burial. Can't believe this is happening. Nightmare. Devastation. Pain.

Trying to get to the other side of the funeral was sheer agony. It took every ounce of energy just to exist. Trying to capture every trace of memory depleted my capacity to function. For months to follow, I watched myself, in slow motion, picking up the shattered glass—-one piercing sliver at a time.

This is where I am.

Fragmented. Soul exposed. Fragile heart.

i grieve

**This pain.
Pain too deep for tears.
Pain that lodges itself underneath
the deepest parts
of my soul
as it whispers,
"Look at me."**

At this, Job got up and tore his robe ... then he fell to the ground in worship and said: 'Naked I came from my mother's womb, and naked I will depart. The Lord gave and the Lord has taken away; may the name of the Lord be praised.'
Job 1:20-21 NIV

i

i . . .

. . . am in a dark place

. . . don't know how i got here

. . . have lost my way

. . . can't wrap my mind around it

. . . am brought to my knees

So many questions during periods of tragedy. I started and ended my days with many. Some answers will be obvious. Some will never be revealed. Still so many questions. One of the most agonizing is "Why?"

Why?

Why has this happened?
Where do I begin?
How do I go on?

What do I say?
When do I know?
Which way do I go?

Who do I turn to?
Why do I cry?
Why . . .

Why?

God sees the big picture. I am not God.

Some days, I can be in the middle of the most mundane task. Then, out of nowhere, I just cry.

i cry

i cry
every time
i think about it

tears of grief
tears of sadness
tears from my soul
i cry

i sometimes try
not to, but
sometimes
i just cry

Be merciful to me, O Lord for I am in distress; my eyes grow weak with sorrow, my soul and my body with grief.

Psalm 31:9 NIV

Going to sleep and waking up—the two most difficult times of existing. During those times, the mind is not anesthetized by the business of living. Therefore, the mind is free to think and drink the tall glass of grief, straight down.

Another Day

I woke up
And realized
With the sunrise
That it was going to be
Another day
Without you

As the day goes on
And the sun sets
It firmly cements
The fact that
Another day
Has gone by without you

Grief, once introduced, must be embraced.

There are certain days when I feel as if I am drowning in a sea of deep, colorless disappointment.

<u>The darkness</u>

What is one to do
with a soul that is
dry,
depleted,
discouraged,
and
depressed?

An existence that is
in disbelief,
disgraced,
disjointed,
dismembered,
disillusioned,
and
displaced?

What is one to do
with a life
discontinued?

***There is no darkness so deep that God's
light cannot reach***

In the still darkness in the middle of the night, I often find myself awake—thinking, feeling, praying, and bandaging my soul. In order to deal with grief, often I have to pick myself up from the ground, look grief squarely in the eyes, shake its hands, and whisper, "Hello."

Still

Still struggling
Still trying to accept
Still want to go back
and change it

Still angry
Still sad
Still wish I would've,
could've, should've . . .

Still praying
Still crying
Still wondering why
Still waiting for an answer
The purpose, the big picture

Still hurting
Still aching
Still

My comfort in my suffering is this: Your promise preserves my life.

Psalm 119:50 NIV

i accept

**God grant me the serenity
to accept the things I cannot change;
the courage to change the things I
can; and the wisdom to know the
difference.**

Reinhold Neibuhr

My mind sees her everywhere I go. I am somewhere between imagining she is here and knowing she is not.

Everywhere I go

Everywhere I go
I see you there
At the park
In the car
In the yard

Running, playing
In my dreams
Laughing, smiling
In my thoughts

A million moments
will pass by and
Everywhere I go
There you are

No matter how much time passes, "what happened" remains a part of you. You must simply learn how to handle it with care.

Some things are meant to be beautiful just for a little while . . . like flowers in full bloom or a breathtaking sunrise. We must enjoy them while they are in the midst of their beauty.

God's Garden

God has this garden
With flowers with the most brilliant
Colors you ever did see
Because He knows everything
He knew what He would do

Ahh,

He then looked down on Earth
And saw the most beautiful
  sunflower
You ever did see

He plucked that beautiful sunflower
Out of the garden of sadness in this
  world

And placed the sunflower very
   carefully
In His garden
With all the other beautiful flowers
And that sunflower shined so
   brightly
With the most brilliant color you
   ever did see

And we know that all things work together for good to them that love God, to them who are called according to His purpose.

Romans 8:28 KJV

Gone 2 Soon

2 birthdays celebrated
2 holidays enjoyed
2 years of memories
2 families destroyed

2 far away to help
2 little time remained
2 sad, 2 painful

Gone, like a faint whisper
Gone 2 soon

Gone at tender 2

Always trust God's perfect timing

As the days lingered by, I noticed that time just kept moving on. People around me continued making plans, living and enjoying life. I realized my plans would be altered forever. It is during those times that I realize how vividly I miss her.

Miss You

Miss you, yes I do
Don't know how
to make it through

If the clock would just go back
And tell me somehow
that this would happen
I would do everything
I could do
to make it go away

Miss you
Yes I do
More than I can say

My thoughts magnify my memories, searching for those moments. Those moments I didn't know would be the last. When I locate the moments, I replay them in my mind over and over and over again.

You never know

You never know
When it will be the
Last kiss you will give
Hug you will get
Smile you will see
Laugh you will hear
Hurt you will heal
Touch you will feel
Treasure them all
When they are real
You just never know

Live each day as if it were your last.
Live a life of few regrets.

i reflect

sometimes the power of a moment captures me and I reflect upon it and am reminded . . .

The power of the pain
Drenches like rain
Embraces the blame
Conceals the shame

Darkness came
Tragedy's gain
The power of the pain
Remains the same

Reflections

Eight weeks later . . .

I still had not unpacked the suitcases from the funeral. Unpacking would acknowledge that "it" did actually happen. It would mean I would have to let go. I don't want to let go. I don't know how. I just don't know how.

Eight months later . . .

Here I am. I can barely open my eyes to see where I am going. I don't know this place. I don't know where I am. I don't know these people. I don't know that person in the mirror. Where am I?

Memories of past, present . . . .

Along with savoring every trace of her beautiful memory, I will always be left wondering what she would have looked like at age 6, 14, 21, 33, 41 . . . .

Never got to

You never got to
Write your name
Ride a bike
Go to school
Learn to swim

You never got to
See the Statue of Liberty
Learn to drive
Fall in love
Get married
Have children
Be a grandma
Celebrate your third birthday
You never got to

And suddenly your breath is taken away. The sight of a sunset. The feel of a cool breeze. The awesomeness of a grand landscape. The smile of a precious child.

<u>Smile</u>

That smile
For a while
Touched us all in a way
That could never
Be explained

That smile
So pure
So free
Teaching us how to be
And will live on
for eternity . . .
That smile

Finally, brethren, whatsoever things are true, whatsoever things are honest, whatsoever things are just, whatsoever things are pure, whatsoever things are lovely, whatsoever things are of good report; if there be any virtue, and if there be any praise, think on these things.

Philippians 4:8 KJV

One of my favorite places in the world is the beach. I like to walk along the beach and enjoy the peacefulness that it brings. Listening to the waves is like God singing a love song to you.

<u>This Summer</u>

This summer
I wanted to take you to the beach
So you could feel the sand in between your toes
And see how high the kite goes
Collect seashells and
watch the sunset turn the ocean gold

This summer
I wanted to build sandcastles with you
And watch the waves wash them away
Write our names in the sand
Run along the shore as fast as we can
This summer

God's Little Sunflower

Many are the plans in a human heart, but it is the Lord's purpose that prevails.

Proverbs 19:21 TNIV

We all have places to put special things so they can be retrieved when needed. Sometimes a special place is needed to rest things that are too overwhelming to handle at the present time. It needs to be placed somewhere to be dealt with . . . later.

The special pink box

There is a special pink box
Where I place my thoughts of
    you
The box—it shines and sparkles
And brightens up a room
The same way you used to

The sad thoughts
Regrets
Happy memories
The missing you

Are captured by each drop of tear
And neatly placed in
That special pink box

Sometimes the pain is too powerful, tears too drenching, and the grief too great. Give it to God.

__i write__

As the sun rises,
my soul groans
These are the words
I write . .

My Journal Entries

I had to write.
Next to prayer, it was the only
constructive outlet I had.
I could express whatever I was feeling
at the time, no barriers. It was during
those times I heard my soul actually
groaning, sometimes screaming. My
letters to God helped cultivate an intimate relationship with Him.

God's Little Sunflower

14 Feb 2006

Dear God,

Happy Valentine's Day. Can't believe almost two weeks have passed since I have written. Today is the day around the country that is marked by the celebration of love and everything that goes along with it. I am so thankful that You died for me to show me what the true meaning of love is. I am so thankful for John 3:16. I am so thankful that You are the Lover of my soul and You are changing me each day to become more and more like You. You are indeed my Valentine because You are the only one I can count on no matter what happens.

17 Feb 2006

Dear God,

Thank You from the bottom of my heart for this time during the past few days. I have received the much needed rest that I have been avoiding, and I have completed some projects that I have been putting on the back burner. I have been doing some soul searching and have come to the realization that all I need is You. . .

05 Mar 2006

Dear God,

As you know, I lost my dear Diovanni a few days ago. I feel like I am dying inside slowly. Making arrangements to bury her was excruciating. I now have to drudge through the days until I can get to the other side of the funeral. I don't think I can take much more of this unbearable pain. I never thought that something like this could devastate me to such a point that I feel as if my heart is literally breaking in two . . .

11 Mar 2006

Dear God,

I just buried my grandbaby yesterday. The hardest thing I have ever had to do. I can't stand it, not even the thought of it. Thank You for giving me the strength during that time of need. There is nothing else I can say at this time. I am out of thoughts, out of emotions, out of tears.

15 Mar 2006

Dear God,

It was not a good morning. I felt my heart breaking in two. I still can't believe she is gone. I do not know what I should be doing. I am numb. The sun is setting as I am writing this sentence. It is a beautiful sunset. Pastel colors across a baby blue sky. Another day gone. Thank You for seeing me through one more day. I feel a sense of peace that I know only comes from You. Help me to lean on You.

17 Mar 2006

Dear God,

Two weeks have gone by and I am still left wondering "What happened?" "How could this happen?" And the ever popular "Why?" No matter how much sorting, reorganizing, and rehashing I do, I still can't fully wrap my mind around it. I am forever changed by this event. I hope for the better. I do not want to be an angry and bitter person. . . .

26 Mar 2006

Dear God,

Here I am again. Still can't believe this has happened. It won't leave me. I don't know how to make it not take me over. Why is my granddaughter gone? I just can't stand it. I know all about trusting in You and the fact that she is in a better place, and all of that, but I just can't connect the dots. I just don't know how to continue to be. How do I go on? How? God, I hate this place I am in. I really hate this. I need Your help in a bad way. This is so hard to deal with.

30 Mar 2006

Dear God,

Not a good day today. It was a month ago today when "it" happened. It happened. I have the spirit of depression. Dreams and hopes are gone and just not wanting to go on seems doable. I feel like Job. Just let me die with ashes on my head . . .

03 Apr 2006

Dear God,

A new month. A new realization that time has passed by and will continue to do so. I just can't stand the pain. I know that You do not give me more than I can bear, but this is a tough one. I can hardly keep from imploding. I am disappointed, disillusioned, and disgusted. I can't keep myself from talking about things I should leave alone. I want so much for the pain to go away and for others to hurt, to feel the pain, the emptiness I feel. The lack of love I feel. I am hurting. I miss Diovanni. I miss her!!

05 Apr 2006

Dear God,

It was about a year ago when we took Diovanni to New Orleans. Now both are gone as we know them. It has still been hard dealing with this place I am in. There is a lot of darkness in here. I can't see my way out. I have had some peace since I have decided not to discuss it anymore and stop all the calls and conservations concerning the matter. There is no more that needs discussing at this point in time. I am so drained. So emotionally drained. I can't function at times. Please help me not to be a bitter and angry person. I don't want to hate. I just want the pain to go away.

So for now, please carry me, because I can't find my way right now. I feel very detached from my family, my feelings, my life. I don't know how to be. I just don't know how to be. Please help me.

10 Apr 2006

Dear God,

Time is moving on and every now and then I find myself latching on to the fact that it is real. She is gone. The nightmare really did happen. I find myself not wanting to talk to others who might ask me questions, make me relive the nightmare. Now I am left writing a book about it. Can you believe that!? A book?!! I would give anything, everything to have her here with me again. I would get rid of it all.

p.s. My soul has been severed to the point of numbness. I am in this place.

I am gonna be here for a while. A long while.

20 Apr 2006

Dear God,

It really helped during counseling yesterday. Even though I felt confident about my feelings going into the session, I soon realized just how raw my pain still is. I have found comfort in leaning on You. I must stay focused on You because the pain freezes me in my tracks when I feel its grip. I actually have to take a deep breath and clench my lips and remember, this is real indeed.

28 Apr 2006

Dear God,

Yesterday was eight weeks ago since "it" happened. In my mind, I walked through the wilderness with her, holding her hand. I saw a beautiful bright light that she walked into as she turned around to wave at me. Now I must turn around and walk back through the wilderness by myself. She is smiling and waving at me. She is happy to be going where she is going. I am sad because I am not going with her. I know I will see her again one day. Then I will never have to leave her. Please help me to go on with my life and not to be a bitter person.

29 Apr 2006

Dear God,

Today I felt like I was away from everything. It's good to get away.. . . . I can't believe I have to live with this in my life, but I do. It is now a part of me, whether I want it to be or not. I couldn't have written a nightmare more horrific. Every time I think about it, I cringe. It makes me want to throw up. My beautiful granddaughter, buried in a tiny casket, in a dress that she was to be wearing to Sunday school this past Easter. I just want to throw up. I am sick to my stomach.

08 May 2006

Dear God,

As the days go by, my grief less intensifies to the point where I can at least function for a while without mentally breaking down. I was at an outing this weekend, and I so wanted her to be there. It was a yearning I could hardly stand. As the days roll forward, I realize the time I will see her again gets closer and closer. I can look at it that way. I have to look at it that way. I just have to.

09 May 2006

Dear God,

It's been two months since I buried my granddaughter. I guess she's really not coming back. I thought maybe I would wake up and realize it was all a long nightmare. Don't think so. Too raw. Too deep. So now my reality is with me everywhere I go. Thank You. I will praise You in the storm.

25 May 2006

Dear God,

My days seem to be going by fast. Can't believe this is almost the middle of the year already. 2006 has been a defining year for me so far. Major events have happened. Roads have been taken. I am still trying to see the good in the tragedy. I can't see it. You know it's there. I wish You would show me. It's funny the lessons you learn as you get older. About life. About people.

04 Jun 2006

Dear God,

It's been three months now since Diovanni's death. My grief is still raw only covered by busyness. Sometimes I break into an inner anguish for no particular reason. I feel "it" on me, like a wet blanket. I know it will never go away from my soul. It is engrained. I am still in the wilderness somewhere. I am not sure exactly where I am. At least I am able to smile. Sometimes.

11 Jun 2006

Dear God,

For some reason, it has been a hard week. At times I just start crying out of nowhere. A verse was asked to be read during Bible study, a comment was made, a certain type of music was playing. I feel so helpless, so empty, so raw. Why am I here in this place of silent grey? I can't go back, I try, but it just agonizes me. At times I can hear my soul screaming. I sometimes feel as if others around me can hear it. How did we get to this point? How did we get here? How? How does a life press forward with passion after such destruction?

13 Jun 2006

Dear God,

I am slowly learning to move on. Slowly. It's hard to be somewhere between moving on and dying inside. It's just hard.

10 Jul 2006

Dear God,

Sometimes I am afraid to be alone with my thoughts. I am afraid of what I might think or how much I think about. Sometimes when I don't think about "it," I am alright. At times when I do think about "it," I am gripped with grief. A fist-clenching grief. I don't know how to deal with this memory that I will no doubt take to the grave with me.

14 Jul 2006

Dear God,

At this point in my life, I am depressed.

24 Jul 2006

Dear God,

It's been a tough week. I can still see the sun on the horizon, and it is still very beautiful.

01 Aug 2006

Dear God,

Time has moved on and every once in a while I am gripped by a moment. I go through it. I embrace it. I let it go. I must go on. I must. I must face this head on, or it will crush me into tiny dust particles. One day I will see why this has come to be.

21 Aug 2006

Dear God,

At times, I feel as if I am on a carnival ride. Sometimes enjoying it. Sometimes not. I feel like I am moving in slow motion.

09 Sep 2006

Dear God,

I thought about Diovanni a lot yesterday. She came to me in a dream. I was so happy to see her. I was just so happy to see her. Then she told me goodbye and went back to sleep. I miss her. I yearn for her. I ache for her.

19 Sep 2006

Dear God,

Not quite sure how to put into words what happened at Port Aransas this past weekend, but You know. Thank You so much for touching me in a special way. I will never forget that Sunday morning sunrise. A miracle sunrise.

27 Sep 2006

Dear God,

Thank You God for the little miracle today. I need them. I am tired and worn out emotionally. Sometimes I am so dazed. I can't think straight.

07 Oct 2006

Dear God,

Thank you God for helping me cope with this reality. The reality that my granddaughter is gone. The reality that at times I smile when I don't feel like it. I am praising You in the storm.

10 Nov 2006

Dear God,

In his grief, Job wanted to give in, to be freed from his discomfort, and to die. But God did not grant Job's request. He had a greater plan for him. To trust God in the good times is commendable, but to trust Him during the difficult times tests us to our limits and exercises our faith. LASB notes

14 Nov 2006

Dear God,

Another day here in my depression. I am dealing with it hour by hour. God is still all powerful and will use this for His greater purpose.

Thanksgiving Day 2006

Dear God,

It was a bitter sweet day. It was hard to see families together. Sometimes it is just too much. I am like this little bug in a big world, trying to make my way to somewhere. I just don't know where. Jesus, please pray for me, because I feel I just can't even pray anymore.

27 Nov 2006

Dear God,

I am in a battle. A serious spiritual battle. I am somewhere between isolation and evaporation. Running on empty. Watching my life like a movie. At times I want to hide because I feel everyone is looking at me and my wounds. Me and my bleeding wounds.

30 Nov 2006

Dear God,

Another month has come to an end. Time goes by quickly. Had a meltdown the other day. Have a lot going on. God, You know better than anyone else that I am having a difficult time. Sometimes, I just kind of don't want to be here.

05 Dec 2006

Dear God,

As I am graveling in grief, rolling around in regret, and dwelling in despair, I can still hear my soul groaning . . . weeping . . . tearing.

Christmas Day 2006

Dear God,

Walking through this holiday was very painful. Did not feel like celebrating the way we use to. Just wanted to rest, relax, and reflect. Still hurts when I think about all that has happened. I think I could handle just about anything except this terrible tragedy. She was with me during the holidays last year. How was I to know it would be the last time?

28 Dec 2006

Dear God,

About to close the door on what has proven to be a most pivotal year in my life. I have learned that there is no use complaining or feeling sorry for myself. I must take the focus off of myself and turn my eyes upon Jesus. You are my only hope. I have no other way out.

New Year's Day 2007

Dear God,

A new year. Trying to find a new normal. Praying that Your will be done in 2007 as in 2006. Thank You for the grace and strength to endure one of the most difficult years I have ever had.

20 Jan 2007

Dear God,

She would have been three today. She gets to spend her birthday with You. She is blessed.

03 Mar 2007

Dear God,

A year has gone by. A year ago today. I was in such agony. I could hardly recognize myself. I was alone in a hotel room. Alone with the thought that I had just seen my granddaughter being unplugged from life support. Gone. She was gone and there was nothing I could do about it. Nothing. I just groaned until I was out of everything. Tonight I am sad, but a peaceful kind of sad. Thank You for Your grace and mercy through this. Thank You.

i survive

With each sunrise
I awoke to the reality
that I was left here for a reason

Who is that lady?

Who is that lady?
Why is she crying . . .
                dying inside?

What could have happened
To break her heart into tiny parts?
She's asking me to help her
I don't know how

Who is that lady?
Gazing back at me, in the mirror
One tragedy older
Doing everything she can
To hold on for dear life

She will soon realize
She must go on
And so her journey
Will begin step

                by

                      step

*"See! The winter is past; the rains are
over and gone.
Flowers appear on the earth;
the season of singing has come, the
cooing of the doves is heard
in our land."*

Song of Solomon 2:11-12 NIV

*"When you least expect it, the Lord
brings people into your life that are
living, walking and talking, "flowers".
They have a beauty that
just takes your breath away.
They stand out in the field of life and
cause you to lift up your heart in
praise to God. They give you hope and
encouragement like seeing the first
flowers of spring."*

*A special devotion from
Chaplain Lyle E. Von Seggern
March 23, 2006*

Bible Chapter Dedication upon the occasion of Diovanni's birth

---

Psalm 20
New International Version

May the LORD answer you
when you are in distress;
may the name of the God
of Jacob protect you.

May he send you help from the sanctuary
and grant you support from Zion.

May he remember all your sacrifices
and accept your burnt offerings.

Selah

May he give you the desire of your heart
and make all your plans succeed.

We will shout for joy when you are victorious and will lift up our banners
in the name of our God.
May the LORD grant all your requests.

Now I know that the LORD
saves his anointed;
he answers him from his holy heaven
with the saving power of his right hand.

Some trust in chariots and some in horses,
but we trust in the name of the LORD our God.

They are brought to their knees and fall,
but we rise up and stand firm.

O LORD, save the king!
Answer us when we call!

Eight things I learned during my grief journey

- *No one has the right to tell me how long it takes to grieve.*

- *It's ok to be sad, mad, angry . . .*

- *It's ok to not feel guilty when I catch myself smiling . . . laughing, crying.*

- *Most of the time, other people just won't understand where I am emotionally. God does.*

- *God is always there.*

- *I will have to find a new normal— a new way of existing.*

- *Life is fragile; handle with prayer.*

- *God has a wonderful plan for my life. I must trust Him.*

Proverbs 3:5-6

Romans 8:28

Jeremiah 33:3

James 1:2-3

Jeremiah 29:11

Psalm 23

Words from a humbled heart

As time went on, I realized that my purpose is to glorify God, no matter what the circumstances dictate. This realization did not take the reality of the pain away, but it gave me a sense of hope. It became my personal ministry to help others on their grief journey, by offering the encouragement and hope God gave to me. With what I experienced and learned, I was better able to be used by God to turn my daughter's focus toward the Son during the last year of her life.**

In time, God's mercy and grace began to mend my broken heart with the kind of love, peace, and joy that only comes from knowing and walking with Him. It is my prayer that my struggle and triumphs can direct others to the only true source of comfort, Jesus Christ.

As I continue to travel on my journey, I have learned to celebrate through the pain.

I celebrate when the sun is shining and when it's pouring rain.
I celebrate when i feel well and when i am gridlocked in pain.
I celebrate when things are fine and during moments of struggling.
I celebrate when i see clearly and when i don't see a thing.
I celebrate when i have victory and when disappointment has its fame.
I celebrate when i have it all and when i have nothing to my name.
I celebrate during moments of joy and when the depths of my soul groan.
I celebrate my life here on Earth and finally, one day, celebrate Home.

P.A.Miller

**Note
Before the completion of this book, I would again walk through the valley of the shadow of death. I would experience the death of my only child Taneesha Deshon (Diovanni's mother). Taneesha is now with Diovanni in the loving arms of the Savior, Jesus Christ. Taneesha is survived by her precious daughter, Serenity.

About the Author

Princess Miller resides in beautiful San Antonio, Texas where she is an active member of Summit Christian Center. She is a graduate of Texas State University in San Marcos, Texas. She has a passion for writing, photography, reading, and traveling around the world with her husband, David. Their travels recently took them on a ten-day spiritual journey to the Holy Land, Israel.

After the death of her granddaughter, God placed on her heart to write *God's Little Sunflower*. This is her first published work and she is currently working on her next writing project "*When Butterflies Fly Away,*" a thirty-one day grief journey devotional inspired by the life and loving memory of her daughter, Taneesha.

Her life's mission statement is to *know, love, and serve God with all her heart, mind, and soul through a passionate, personal relationship with Jesus Christ—the Prince of Peace.*

Her life's verse is Proverbs 3:5-6. *Trust in the Lord with all your heart and lean not on your own understanding; In all your ways acknowledge Him, and He shall direct your paths.* NKJV

She is the founder of *Project Sunflower*—a ministry offering hope and encouragement in the midst of grief. Through this ministry, she hopes to encourage those on their grief journey to hold on . . . no matter what, by turning to the only true source of comfort—Jesus Christ. She gives all the glory, honor, and praise to Him for His presence in her life.

For more information on Project Sunflower, visit www.projectsunflower.net

God loves you.
He sent His only Son, Jesus Christ
to die for you.
When you receive Christ into your
heart, you become a child of God.
You now have a personal relationship
with Jesus Christ

How to receive Jesus Christ

- Admit you are a sinner
- Be willing to turn from your sins (repent)
- Believe that Jesus died on the cross and rose from the grave.
- Through prayer, invite Jesus to come in and control your life

through the Holy Spirit. (Receive Him as Lord and Savior)

Prayer of Salvation

Dear Lord Jesus, I know that I am a sinner and need You as my Savior. I believe You died for my sins. I need Your forgiveness. I invite You to come into my heart and life. I trust You as my Lord and Savior. I give my life to You. In Jesus' name. Amen.

www.ingramcontent.com/pod-product-compliance
Ingram Content Group UK Ltd.
Pitfield, Milton Keynes, MK11 3LW, UK
UKHW041943230426
12048UKWH00008B/109